I0755798

Taking Care of Little Snoogie

A Story About Pet Loss for Adults

Written by Peggy A. Rothbaum, Ph.D.,
Stefanie Worwag, VMD, DAVCIM, and
Jonathan C. Goodwin, DVM, MS, DACVIM-Cardiology

Illustrations by Tim Mullen

Printed in the U.S.A.

Taking Care of Little Snoogie: A Story About Pet Loss
for Adults written by Peggy A. Rothbaum,
Stefanie Worwag, and Jonathan C. Goodwin

Layout by Mullen Design, LLC
Illustrations by Tim Mullen
Photography courtesy of the authors

ISBN 978-0-9883592-0-8

Visit us on Facebook:
https://www.facebook.com/TakingCareOfLittleSnoogie

Paws4Animals LLC
232 Saint Paul Street
Westfield, NJ 07090
paws4animalsllc@gmail.com

Dedication

We dedicate this book:

To pets and their people everywhere. We hope for loving homes for all pets.

To Dr. Jennifer Bruce, who took care of Little Snoogie in her younger years.

To the kind pharmacists at Tiffany Natural Pharmacy (Westfield, NJ) who compounded all of those medications, often on short notice, so that Little Snoogie could have what she needed.

To all of the fabulous people at Garden State Veterinary Specialists (Tinton Falls, NJ) who helped us to take care of Little Snoogie: Drs. Avery Kasten, Sarah Round, and Lucy Hanus, Ms. Kristy Garcia, the internal medicine and cardiology technicians, and the incredibly kind front desk staff who greeted Little Snoogie with affection and concern at all hours of the day and night.

And, of course, to Gloria.

"No heaven will not ever heaven be, unless my cats are there to welcome me."

— Anonymous

Foreword

As a young boy with an uncanny ability to toss a ping-pong ball into a fish bowl, my room contained a goldfish or two whenever a carnival or street fair came to town.

The fish lived for a week, died, received the standard goldfish burial service and then were eventually replaced. No crying, no tears. There were no emotional ties with the many fish I owned, certainly not like the strong feelings I had for my baseball cards.

Lose a fish, win a new one.

Why then do pet owners grieve over the loss of a pet? I didn't get it.

Maybe time together is the answer. Over time a bond forms and a relationship builds. The pet provides companionship; sometimes makes you laugh when a laugh is really needed and sometimes your pet is just a nonjudgmental friend. When your pet becomes a member of the family, the loss of that family member is cause to grieve.

The loss is cherished and irreplaceable.

I, a casual owner of goldfish, never understood the grief. Then one day I was introduced to

Little Snoogie. Her antics were amusing and for no apparent reason her trips to the vet became a source of my concern.

This is a book about the life and times of Little Snoogie, someone's companion, friend and family member. She left her paw print on our hearts.

— Joseph P. Paluscio, CPA, MST*

*The authors thank Joe for suggesting that we write this book and for his help and encouragement throughout the process.

Little Snoogie was a cat. She lived until she was 15½ years old.

Little Snoogie selected her person, Peggy, at St. Hubert's Animal Welfare Center in Madison, New Jersey. She was their cat #10,329.

Little Snoogie's future godmother, Sharon, was there too. But Little Snoogie was a smart kitty. Pretty soon she figured out that Peggy was the one who was there to get kitties. So, she started paying a lot of attention to Peggy. She jumped on her lap and snuggled up to her.

Sharon said, "You have to take this cat home. You have no choice. She has picked you. Look at her."

So, Little Snoogie went home with Peggy and another cat, Catbaby. Catbaby was St. Hubert's cat #10,403. Catbaby and Little Snoogie lived together for the rest of Little Snoogie's life.

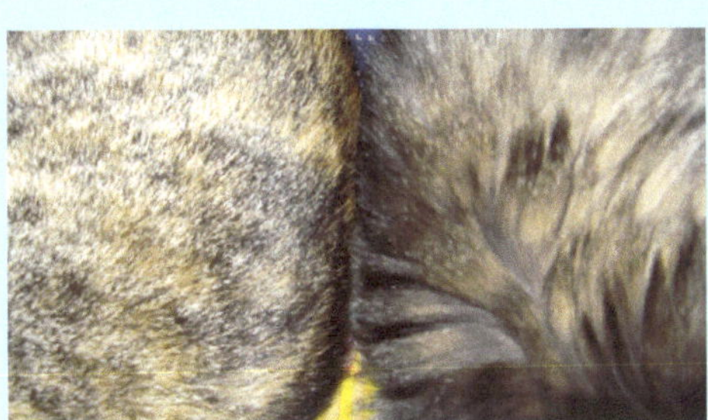

They kind of tolerated each other.

Little Snoogie didn't feel well for a lot of her life. She was cranky.

Then she met Dr. Worwag, and her life got much better.

Little Snoogie needed some adjustments to her therapy for her intestines and some new medication to treat her hyperactive thyroid gland. This is Dr. Worwag's specialty, so she was able to help Little Snoogie, although Little Snoogie was not exactly a willing and cooperative patient.

"Little Snoogie was quite a character. She was like an affectionate little fireball. She tolerated us up to a certain point. She surely did let us know when she had enough of us."

Little Snoogie had to take some pills and see the cat cardiologist, Dr. Goodwin, too.

"Little Snoogie's heart may be sick, but her desire to go on is very healthy. She may be little, but Snoogie is tough! Little Snoogie has a problem with her thyroid gland that will cause her to lose weight even when she eats and may cause her to be grumpy (EXTRA grumpy when Catbaby is around!). What we will do is start medication to help protect Little Snoogie's heart from the aggressive effects of her thyroid disease. If her disease continues to progress, we can give her a shot that will cure her thyroid disease. We will continue to watch Snoogie closely to see how she is doing."

Turns out that Little Snoogie was a very sweet cat!

Little Snoogie liked to sleep in her catnest.

Little Snoogie took over the whole house.

"Everything you see here is mine."

Little Snoogie was very determined.

Little Snoogie was funny too.

She followed Peggy, her person, all around. Peggy knew about how Dr. Konrad Lorenz had shown that animals, like ducks, will bond with and follow around an adopted mother of a different species. When it was time to eat, Peggy would say "Ducks!!!" and Little Snoogie would get up and follow Peggy to EEEAAAATTTT!!! Catbaby always followed right after Little Snoogie.

Little Snoogie was a very picky eater.

She only ate salmon with chunks and gravy.

Little Snoogie was your basic rooster kitty. As soon as it got light she would say Roooouuwwwwhhh Roooouuwwwwhhh in a low, throaty voice. Gradually it got very high-pitched and louder and louder:

Roooouuwwwwhhh!!!
Roooouuwwwwhhh!!!
Roooouuwwwwhhh!!!
Roooouuwwwwhhh!!!

Little Snoogie was ready to begin her day!

Peggy, Little Snoogie's person, often had to drive her to the hospital late at night when she got home from work. Little Snoogie's health problems just kept flaring up. Peggy didn't want Little Snoogie to get worse or to be in pain overnight. Dr. Hanus was often the veterinarian who worked the night shift. It was always such a relief to see Dr. Hanus, because Peggy trusted her and she was always so calm. When Little Snoogie needed to be hospitalized, Dr. Worwag and Dr. Hanus tried to get her home as soon as possible.

Dr. Worwag said "Even though Little Snoogie became a very nice cat, she still kept her spicy and feisty character." Little Snoogie complained and carried on when she was in the hospital. As Dr. Hanus put it once: "Little Snoogie doesn't like it here anymore and would do much better at home."

Then Little Snoogie really began to get sick.

Little Snoogie's appetite decreased. Her kidney function weakened and she developed a urinary tract infection. Despite thorough treatment, she did not improve. Little Snoogie continued to eat less and less and became thinner and thinner.

Peggy did not want to lose Little Snoogie.

She kept hoping that Little Snoogie would get well.

Dr. Worwag tried very hard to help Little Snoogie. But finally she said, "She has only a few days, at most, left."

Peggy, Little Snoogie's person, loved Little Snoogie so much. She was holding Little Snoogie and crying. She said, "But these kind of days are no good."

But Peggy refused to let Little Snoogie suffer.

Dr. Worwag said, "There is one important thing that we can do for our beloved companions. We can let them go peacefully, controlled, with their owner present and holding them. We don't want our best friend to suffer."

"It is one of the hardest things to do, to put your cat, dog or any other species to sleep. Your pet is a family member and it is an awful feeling to make a decision about life and death. But at the end, things only continue to get worse and I believe it is important that we look at the quality of life of our companions and do not let them suffer. Nevertheless, it is only little comfort to know that it is the right decision so that your beloved friend does not suffer anymore."

So, Little Snoogie died peacefully in Peggy's arms around 5:30 pm on Thursday, April 28, 2011. It was just Peggy, their beloved Dr. Worwag, and Little Snoogie. Peggy and Little Snoogie had a great last weekend, but she started to decline over the week.

Anneliese, Little Snoogie's animal healer, helped all week. So did her cat sitter, who came by when Peggy was at work. John checked the car out, so that Peggy could be sure of getting down and back from Tinton Falls on Snoogie's last ride.

On her last day, Little Snoogie and Peggy spent the whole day together snoozing, cuddling, and chatting on the bed. Sometimes Catbaby joined them. Although Little Snoogie was uncomfortable, she was not in pain. Peggy watched her fade throughout the day. By the end of the day, not only had she stopped eating, but she had stopped her previously incessant water drinking. She was starting to have a little trouble keeping her balance. She was more and more quiet and slept more and more. Peggy believed that she was not afraid until she put Little Snoogie in her carrier. She fought Peggy on that. She was such a fighter, as she had not felt totally well for most of her 15½ years. This made it more heartbreaking, but her health was only going to get worse. She was clearly not going to give up, so Dr. Worwag and Peggy had to help her. She would have suffered very much if they hadn't done so. They know that they did the right thing, though Peggy will miss Little Snoogie terribly. Catbaby seemed okay, even as she realized that Little Snoogie was not coming back from the hospital this time.

At first, Peggy was so relieved that Little Snoogie wasn't suffering.

But it was such a terrible loss, and she missed Little Snoogie so much.

It just wasn't right.

Little Snoogie was not where she was supposed to be.

Her favorite places were empty. Little Snoogie just wasn't there.

She was everywhere in the house, but nowhere at all.

It was too quiet in the morning.

Peggy was heartbroken.

Losing Little Snoogie brought up other losses of other pets.

And then there were all of those unanswerable questions, such as, "Why did Little Snoogie have to die?"

Catbaby didn't miss Little Snoogie…
AT ALL.

So many people understood how Peggy felt about losing Little Snoogie.

They said kind and comforting words.

Jamie said: “I am so sorry to hear about Little Snoogie.”

Amy said: “i am sorry for ur loss and wll be thinking of you... all of it sounds cliche but if there's anything i cn do- u know the drill but i mean it... love you.”

Jane said: “I am so sorry to hear about Snoogie. I had a similar situation with my black shepherd. It is heart breaking. Of course, time will heal and you will remember the good times over the sorrowful ones, but that does not help you right now. Right now, it is just taking one day at a time. My prayers and thoughts are with you.”

Anneliese, Little Snoogie's animal healer, said: “What I pick up on Snoogie's energy is that she is quite content and happy. As for being around, I don't know exactly with animal spirits, but on the human level, the spirit stays around for a while. I am pretty sure that animals stay around as well, but in the form of something that reminds you of her. Does that make sense to you? You cannot bring Snoogie back, but her spirit is with you. Remember she is in a very good place (kitty heaven) and she is very happy."

Kind people talked to Peggy about how hard it had been for them when their beloved pets were so sick and died. Sometimes it was hard to listen to the stories because they were so sad and painful. However, it also made Peggy feel good because so many people understood and wanted to talk with her about their feelings.

Carol said: "I am so sorry to hear about your loss of Little Snoogie. You have certainly been a wonderful loving mother to her and made her difficult life so much better. I can't think of a better person to have cared for her over her lifetime. If you need some comfort food over the next few days, just let me know. I deliver. Love to you."

Leslie said: "Just wanted you to know that I'm thinking of you and so sorry for your loss. Be in touch when you are ready no matter how long it takes. Xo"

Barbara said: "I'm so sorry to hear about Little Snoogie's passing. I'm glad I got to meet her, even though it was only once. She was so fortunate to have spent her life being loved and cared for by you."

Alex said: "I know how awful it is to lose a pet. My dog died."

Pamela said: "I do know how much you cherished your sweet cat and how hard it is to be without your pet. They comfort silently in a way no person can. The memories are always there as well as the confidence that you were given a life that you loved, protected, and cared for. May you be blessed for this always."

Claire said: "I remember when my puppy died. This animal is like a child, suffering and doesn't know why. I felt the loss as if it was a child. I appreciated the sorrow as it is very deep."

Jill sent an e-card.

Sharon, Little Snoogie's godmother, sent a card that said: "Our kindest thoughts are with you as you grieve the loss of Little Snoogie."

Elaine said: "My condolences." Elaine liked to tell Peggy stories about Mintsie, her grandmother's cat when she was a little girl in the 1930s.

Liz emailed: "I had pets growing up and I remember how heartbroken my father was when our dog passed away. He stayed up with her while she was dying and wouldn't leave her side. So you know where I learned about compassion. Animals are as much a part of us as people. We just got a tortoise and I am so loving him! It doesn't take much."

Joe said: "Your email was heartbreaking."

Some people expressed their feelings without words. Peggy arrived for a lunch meeting with Paula, and Paula gave her a beautiful violet "just because."

Peggy kept thinking that she should donate Little Snoogie's food to Cattitude, Mary's animal charity.

She just couldn't do it.

She kept trying and trying to do it.

Peggy emailed Mary about it: "I thought that I was going to be able to part with Little Snoogie's food today. But I don't think that I am ready yet. What if she comes back and she's hungry? Silly me." (In fact, the night before Thanksgiving the year that Little Snoogie died, Peggy had a dream that Little Snoogie came back and she was hungry! In her dream, Peggy was holding Little Snoogie and Little Snoogie was eating her favorite food! Salmon with chunks and gravy!!!!)

Peggy told Mary, "Maybe Saturday. Not Thursday, although I will be working at home, as it is the 3rd week anniversary of her death. I took her medications to Tinton Falls for some hard working family trying to take care of their cat or the very beloved staff's pets. I have been gathering her belongings together, but I am not ready to part with the food yet. Sooner or later it will occur to me that some other sweet little fur ball at Cattitude can use it."

Mary emailed back and said: "It's a nice thing about Asian religions: they keep putting out bits of food for their departed! Because, as you say, you never know if she will come back and be hungry. As you know, I do believe they come back in a new body but with their same soul."

It was all so heartwarming and comforting.

Peggy just ignored some of the other comments:

It was just a cat.

Get another one.

This is sad, but not tragic.

You should be over it by now.

She was old anyway.

That's not as bad as things that have happened to me.

How sad for these people to never know the sweet love of a pet.

Peggy felt such comfort from all of the kind words from people who care about her and Little Snoogie. She began to do things to comfort herself and hold her memories of Little Snoogie.

She made a memorial box of all of Little Snoogie's stuff, including her green rat.

She made a list of all of her memories of Little Snoogie.

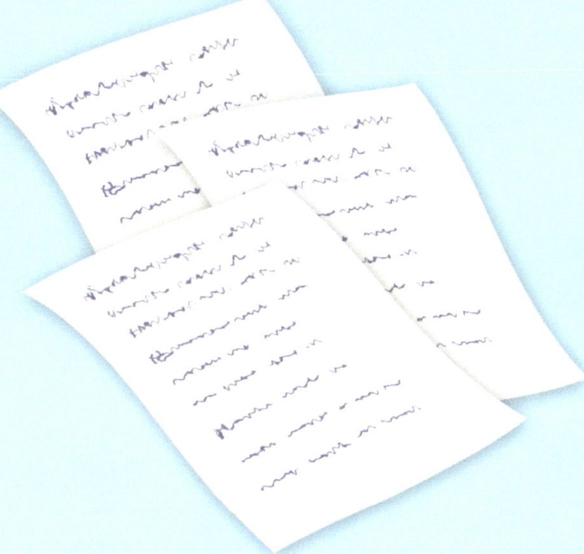

She remembered Little Snoogie doing some of the things that she always did.

She made a “four kitties” quilt.

One day when Peggy was running through Lord and Taylor, she saw a scarf that had all of the colors that Little Snoogie had, and no extra colors!

She bought it!

When Peggy took Catbaby to her next checkup at the hospital, Dr. Goodwin, Dr. Worwag, and other people came in to talk and reminisce about Little Snoogie. They even laughed with some of the memories about how Little Snoogie was such a funny cat. They talked about how she and Gloria had something special right from Little Snoogie's first visit there!

Dr. Worwag said, "We laughed about how Little Snoogie let us know when she had enough of us and how she needed to have her hair mats clipped off from time to time because she did not want to be brushed. She was our feisty Little Snoogie."

Little Snoogie's spirit will live on forever.

She will always be loved.

What we can learn from Little Snoogie:

Appreciate your home.

Try to go home when you need comfort and support.

Live your life to the fullest.

Go to the doctor when you are sick, even if you don't want to go.

Keep on going even if you don't feel good.

Be courageous.

Be determined.

Don't get discouraged.

Keep on fighting.

Never give up.

Be thankful for everyone who helps you along the way.

Dr. Peggy A. Rothbaum is a psychologist, writer and researcher in Westfield, New Jersey. However, a very important additional mission is taking care of cats. Just ask Catbaby.

Dr. Stefanie Worwag was born and raised in Germany. She came to the United States in 1993 to pursue her education. After her bachelor's degree from the University of Notre Dame, she received her VMD in 2001 from the University of Pennsylvania, School of Veterinary Medicine. She completed a small animal rotating internship and her Internal Medicine residency at the Animal Medical Center in New York City in 2004. Dr. Worwag has been a staff internist at Garden State Veterinary Specialists in New Jersey since 2004 and became a Diplomat of The American College of Veterinary Internal Medicine in 2008. She also was trained in Veterinary Acupuncture at the Chi Institute in Reddick, Florida.

Dr. Jonathan C. Goodwin was born and raised in Detroit, Michigan. He attended Cornell University and received a Bachelor's of Science Degree. He then matriculated to Tuskegee University College of Veterinary Medicine for his Doctor of Veterinary Medicine degree. He completed his residency in cardiology at Purdue University. His special interests include congenital heart disease, feline myocardial disease, and management of heart failure.

Acknowledgements

Tim Mullen is an accomplished freelance graphic designer and illustrator. His work can be viewed at be.net/tmullendesign. The authors thank Tim for the design, layout, and beautiful illustrations.

Patrick Sullivan is a freelance writer and editor based in New Jersey. He has written for Patch.com, Black Belt magazine, The NonProfit Times and more." To learn more visit: www.psully.com. The authors thank Patrick for editing and proofreading our manuscript.

www.ingramcontent.com/pod-product-compliance
Lightning Source LLC
LaVergne TN
LVHW071629100826
845154LV00005BA/110

* 9 7 8 0 9 8 8 3 5 9 2 0 8 *